IS HEALTH?

Faith Hill
Gillian Geary

FOOD

Oxford University Press

Phototypeset in Univers and Century Old Style by
Tradespools Limited, Frome, Somerset

Printed by Ebenezer Baylis Limited, Worcester

Acknowledgements

The illustrations are by: **Peter Ahern, Susan
Beresford, Mel Calman, Ed Carr, Nick Duffy,
Gecko Ltd, Jean Hands, Illustra Design, Beverly
Levy, Chris Price, Mike Sharp** and **David Watson**.

The photos were provided by: **Format/Joanne O'Brien**
3 (right), /**Jenny Matthews** 22, (bottom right); /**Frank
Lane Agency** 22 (top left, top centre, top right);
Network/Chris Davies 3 (centre), 23; /**Martin Mayer**
3 (left); **Topham Picture Library** 22 (bottom left); **Rex
Features** 22 (bottom centre).

CONTENTS

Attitudes to **F**ood and **E**ating

Although many people of all ages eat poorly, you often hear adults complaining that young people are the worst. They'll tell you that some young people don't bother much at all with food. Many parents worry about 16 or 17 year-olds when they leave school and seem to give up eating 'proper' meals.

And what about the young people themselves? These are some of the things they say about food. Do you agree with them?

	Agree	**Disagree**

Most of the time I don't have proper meals any more ...

I never bother with breakfast ...

Most of the food in the canteen is junk. But it's there so that's what you eat ...

My Mum leaves food out for me, but I can't be bothered to eat it ...

Even if you know something's bad for you, you still eat it if you like it ...

Eating brown bread and stuff is just posh ...

When you have read through the statements and put in ticks to show whether you agree or disagree, you could discuss your views in a small group. For example:

● Do you agree with what is said?
● Do many of the people you know eat like this?
● Do *you* think it matters what people eat?

What people eat will depend on many different things, including their attitudes towards food and their opinion on the importance of a healthy diet.

❝Cooking is a waste of time.**❞**

❝You need lots of vitamins and proteins**❞**

❝Fresh food is too expensive**❞**

❝You should have a good meal once a day.**❞**

❝I eat when I feel like it**❞**

❝I don't eat pork**❞**

In your group, discuss what the people in these photographs might think about food and eating properly. Do you think their attitudes would be very different? If so, why would they be different? If not, why not?

Of course, in discussing these photos we are just guessing. We can't really know what people think just by looking at them.

ACTIVITY

You could find out what people in your school/college/community actually think about the importance of food by carrying out a survey. As a group you could begin by brainstorming a list of 6 to 10 questions and then using these, write a questionnaire. In pairs, you could then arrange to interview people and fill in the questionnaires with them. These might be people at school or college, other friends or family and/or individuals in a street survey. When you have filled in as many questionnaires as possible, you will need to add up all the results.

Remember:
If you want to look for difference according to age and sex, you'll need to ask for these details on the form.

Remember:
Check with your school/college on their rules about questionnaires and working in the community.

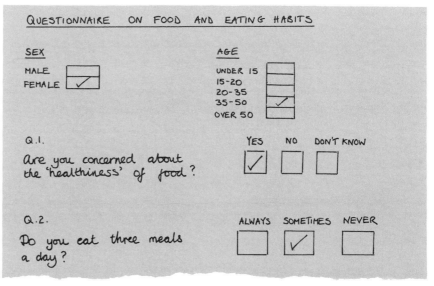

Your group should then get together when the survey is completed, to discuss:

● What you have found out about people's attitudes towards food and eating.

● Whether any of the results are particularly interesting or surprising.

● Whether the survey has influenced your own attitudes to food and eating at all.

Mixed Messages

Where do our attitudes to food come from? It's easy to think, 'That's me, I've always been like that.' Some people feel that their attitudes are fixed and will never change. But people's attitudes *do* change.

One reason why our attitudes change is because we are always gathering different messages. Have you ever thought about the different messages you've received about food and drink from the time you were a baby? Did your mother or father try to make you eat things you didn't like because they were 'good for you'? Were you made to stay at the table until you'd finished something you hated and made you feel sick? Later on, were you more influenced by your friends?

66 *I've never bothered with food . . . I'm not that sort of person.* 99

66 *I've always hated eating . . .* 99

ACTIVITY

This next activity is intended to help you consider the messages you have received all your life about food and drink and to think about how these have influenced you. It may take you up to an hour to complete it and you will need large sheets of flipchart paper or drawing paper and bright-coloured pens.

> Start by working on your own and dividing the flipchart sheet into 6 squares. Each square represents a different stage of your life; the last square being the present stage in your life.

> In each square, draw and write some of the messages which you received at each stage about food and drink. For example, the first square might be 0 to 5 years and you would include some of the messages you got as a small child.

> When you have finished, pair up with another person. Each of you take a turn at explaining and talking through your own sheet, discussing any points that arise. How have the messages influenced *your* feelings about eating and drinking?

> In a larger group, report back on your shared discussions. Consider any points that are interesting or of concern to particular individuals.

Remember:

When you are reporting back, don't repeat anything confidential that your partner has told you.

Media messages

Many of the messages we receive come from advertisements in magazines and from television. Each year the food industry spends more than £200 million on advertising. Most is spent on unhealthy products, such as sweets, chocolates, ice-cream, cakes, etc. How far do you think these advertisements influence our attitudes to food and soft drinks?

If you look closely at a range of adverts for food and soft drinks you will see that they include a number of different messages. Some are quite direct and open, such as: New Zealand lamb is the best! Others are more subtle, hidden messages, such as the idea that you are not a 'good' wife and mother unless you use certain gravy mix or breakfast cereal. Many of these hidden messages are linked to 'stereotypes' about men and women, and family life, e.g. the false image of the 'typical' British family being a white mother and father, with one boy and one girl, living in a very nice house. Very few families are actually like this.

ACTIVITY

> If you collect a pile of magazines you could examine some of these advertisements. Work in pairs and make a list of the messages in food and drink advertisements in the magazines. Look out for ones that include:

Sexy women   'Good' wives/mothers   Pleased/satisfied men
Children   Health claims   Glamour and expense
Any other topics that you think are important.

If you are working in a larger group, each pair could produce a collage of adverts that go with one of these headings. These could be displayed with a list of the messages about the foods, written up alongside.

Of course, it's not only magazines that include food advertisements. You could make a video of TV adverts and analyse them under the same headings. Or you could keep a diary of the TV programmes you watch for one week. How many of these include scenes of people eating and cooking? What messages do they convey about attitudes to food and drink?

> Your group might like to discuss the influence of TV and magazines on people's opinions on food and eating habits. For example:

● Do you feel that magazines and TV are important?
● How easily are people influenced by advertisements?
● One advert may not have much impact, but what about the long-term effects of continued advertising?

How do you feel about the different ways that men and women are presented in relation to food? Does it influence the way women feel about themselves and their attitudes to food? What about the effect on men?

Further Information

1 There is a section on advertising and health in the booklet in this series called, *What is Health?*

2 *Health Matters – the YTS health education resource pack*, published by the National Extension College, includes a section on making sense of health messages and the media.

Eat well.
Crosse & Blackwell.

TWININGS
HERBAL INFUSIONS

The pride of Cornwall

Only one decaffeinated coffee has that golden roasted taste.

'Nescafé Gold Blend'

Listening to Experts

The main advice coming from experts on food and nutrition is that we should cut down on fat, sugar and salt, while increasing the amount of fibre or 'roughage' that we eat. But realistically, how many of us ever take any notice of experts? Some people reject all expert advice, and most of us tend to be a bit cynical when it comes to acting on it. Why do you think this is?

In your group brainstorm all the reasons why people ignore the advice of experts. Then discuss whether or not you agree with any of these reasons.

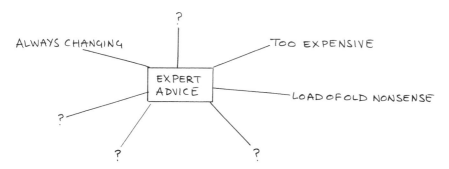

When we are thinking about expert advice there are some important questions that we need to ask.

Who says?

We need to be sure just where advice is coming from. Since the early 1980s there has been a mountain of new advice about food and nutrition. This mountain is made up of reports from specialist working parties. The most important of these is called the NACNE report. NACNE stands for the National Advisory Committee on Nutrition Education, and was set up in 1979 under Professor Jerry Morris. Its findings, which were published in 1984, set out definite targets for changing the British diet.

NACNE advised these changes in the British diet.

How do we know?

The trouble with reports like the one from NACNE is that they are so technical that you need to be an expert to understand them. So most of us have to rely on second-hand advice. And listening to second-hand advice can be a little like buying a second-hand car.

So we need to ask more questions. Like:
● Who is giving us the information?
● Why are they giving it to us?
● What have they got to gain?
● What information are they leaving out?

Which of these would you trust most? Why?
● A newspaper report
● An advice column in a magazine
● A leaflet produced by a food store
● A leaflet produced by the Government's Health Education Authority
● Advice from your own doctor or nurse.

Are they sure?

Even if we are sure that we have got the 'official' advice, how can we know that they have got it right? After all, the advice given about food and eating habits keeps changing and so maybe the experts are only guessing. They can't *prove* that certain foods are bad for you.

This depends a bit on what kind of proof we are looking for. Food experts can't give us the sort of absolute proof you get from a science lab, because it would be so difficult to set up an experiment. You would need to take thousands of new-born babies and place them in two groups. One group would grow up as normal but the other group would have to eat only certain foods for their entire lives and you would have to rule out other factors, such as smoking. Such an experiment would be impossible!

However, there is another sort of proof, based on deductive reasoning. This is the way that criminals are found guilty or not guilty in a law court. The judge and the jury weigh up the evidence each way and then give their verdict. In the same way, experts can look at the evidence regarding diet and declare certain foods 'guilty' or 'not guilty'.

They can use a whole range of different evidence to base their judgements on. For example, the food people eat in different countries. Or the food that was eaten in Britain at different times during history.

New evidence will unfortunately mean that advice *will* change from time to time. Is there any way of avoiding this? Does it mean that we should ignore the best advice there is now?

ACTIVITIES

» Experts agree that during the Second World War people in Britain ate a very healthy diet. Find out as much as you can about wartime food rationing and what people ate during the war. Grandparents and other elderly people may be able to help and your local library probably stocks copies of wartime newspapers which will include advice and menus.

» Carry out research into one or more food products which you plan to put on trial. Some members of your group could plan the case for the defence, researching into the advantages. Others could look at the disadvantages, planning the prosecution. At a previously agreed time, you could hold a mock trial, calling witnesses, with judge and jury, etc. If the outcome is 'guilty', you may decide on a complete ban or just a partial ban on the product as a reduced sentence!

Why We Need Food

We need food to keep the body healthy. Foods that are eaten every day contain different nutrients. These are substances that are needed by the body. Carbohydrates, fats, proteins, vitamins and minerals are all nutrients.

It is important that we eat a variety of foods. Not all foods contain these nutrients so a mixed diet is vital.

Digestion

To be able to make use of the food that we eat it has to be digested. During digestion, food that has been eaten, is broken down by the body into simple parts that can be used by the body.

You could identify the different parts of the digestive system by labelling the arrows on this diagram. Work in small groups and then compare results. If you are interested in the technical terms you could check up on them in a biology text book.

The Digestive System

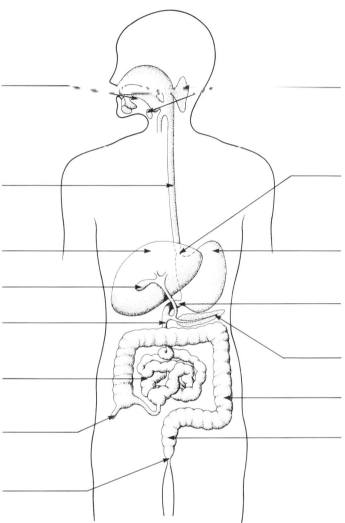

What the different foods are needed for

Nutrients	What they do	Foods in which they are found
Carbohydrates		
Sugars	Sugars are used for energy. Any extra that is not used can be stored as fat which could lead to weight problems. Sugars also cause tooth decay.	Sweets, jam, marmalade, cakes, biscuits, chocolate, canned drinks, fruit drinks, syrup, honey, most tinned fruits.
Starches	Starches are also used for energy. They are more bulky and filling than sugary foods so are less likely to cause weight problems.	Bread, rice, chapatis, pasta, cereals, potatoes, beans, pastry.
Fibre	Fibre adds bulk to our diet. It helps our digestive system to stay healthy.	Fruit and vegetables, cereals, beans, bread, wholemeal products, e.g. pastry, pasta.

Nutrients	What they do	Foods in which they are found
Proteins	Proteins are needed by the body for cell growth and repair. They are found in animal and vegetable form.	Fish, chicken, eggs, cheese, nuts, meat, milk, bread, fruit and vegetables, pulses and beans.
Fats	Fats give our body energy. If too much fat is eaten it can cause weight problems when it is stored in the body. There are two main types of fats:	
Saturated fats	These are found mainly in animal meats and animal products. If they are eaten in large amounts the heart may be damaged.	Butter, eggs, hard margarine, meat, palm oil, ghee, blended oil, coconut oil.
Polyunsaturated fats	These are fats and oils from vegetable products and fish.	Sunflower oil, soya, soft margarine, nuts, fish, olive oil, maize oil, safflower oil.
Vitamins and Minerals	There are a number of different vitamins and minerals which are needed to keep the body healthy and prevent disease.	A variety of foods need to be eaten to obtain the vitamins and minerals that are needed.

ACTIVITY

You might like to find out what general type of diet you eat. Take one day, for example, yesterday, and try to remember everything that you ate and drank. Draw out a chart similar to the one below and quickly record with a tick every time you ate a food containing sugar, starch, fibre, protein, saturated fats and polyunsaturated fats.

An example is given below for breakfast, where a person ate toast with butter and marmalade and drank a cup of tea with milk and sugar. In the chart there will be two ticks for the sugar found in the tea and marmalade, two for saturated fat found in the milk and the butter, one tick for the fibre and starch found in the toast and a tick for the protein found in the bread. You may find the food table above will help you.

Meal	Sugars	Starches	Fibre	Protein	Saturated fats	Polyunsaturated Fats
Breakfast	√√	√	√	√	√√	
Snack						
Midday meal						

After you have had time to complete your chart you could discuss in small groups any problems you found in completing it. For example, some foods, such as pizza could be a combination of at least four different nutrients. Did you find more ticks in some columns than in others? The completed chart should give you some idea of how many times a day you are eating each of these nutrients.

Food, Energy and Exercise

Food and energy

Food that we eat is used to give the body energy. The energy in the food is measured in calories, kilocalories or kilojoules.

The energy is used for many body functions, such as heart beat and breathing, digestion and brain activity.

Other calories are needed for growth, movement and extra exercise.

For example the kilocalorie intake for this person in a day is 2000 kcals. They are fairly active and use all the kcals that they eat.

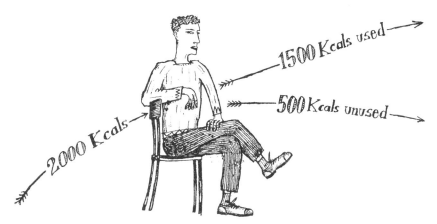

The calories are used as above.

The extra 500 kilocals that are not used, will be stored in the body as fat.

The kilocalorie intake for this person is 2000 kcals in a day. In this case only 1500 kcals are used

To be healthy we need to balance the number of calories eaten with the number used by the body. If we don't get this balance right we could become over- or underweight. Surveys in the UK show that 15 per cent of 15 to 19 year-olds are overweight and 1 per cent are seriously underweight.

ACTIVITIES

» Brainstorm the words linked with fat people and thin people.

Fat people are: HAPPY   Thin people are . . .

Some foods contain more calories than others.	
	Per gram
FATS	9 kilocals
ALCOHOL	7 kilocals
PROTEINS	4 kilocals
CARBOHYDRATES	4 kilocals

Discuss in small groups why you think we use these words. How do you feel about your weight? You could discuss your feelings with your group but don't feel that you have to. Many people are very sensitive about their weight. Why do you think this is?

》 It is possible to check your general weight on a chart as is shown below. If you are interested in your weight you might like to check with the chart. Measuring the weight of a person is not always an accurate way of finding out if they are overfat. This is because muscle is heavy and a very muscular person could appear overweight. To measure the amount of fat on the body a skin fold test can be done. This measures the amount of fat under the skin. You could try to find out more about this test from PE staff.

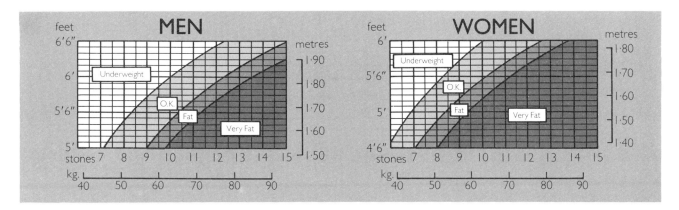

Exercise

Exercise is important to keep the body at the right weight and to stay fit. People also say that they feel better when exercising regularly, not only physically but also mentally.

Fitness is a combination of three things:

1 Stamina

2 Strength

3 Suppleness

Being able to keep going when running or walking quickly without getting tired or out of breath.

Being able to carry, climb stairs, unscrew bottles, etc.

Being able to bend stretch, twist and turn easily.

A fit person is less likely to get injured from strains and sprains. Energetic stamina exercise is important to keep the heart healthy. Exercise for 20 to 30 minutes a day 2 or 3 times a week to keep fit and stay fit.

How fit are you?

You might like to try some of the tests below. Please make sure that you read the warning above before attempting any of the tests.
The tests are not highly scientific. They can only give you a very rough guide to your fitness.

1 *Stamina test*
If you run or jog on the spot you can test the fitness of your leg muscles, lungs and heart. The more you are out of breath after this exercise, the less stamina you have.

Try the stamina test for two minutes to start with. The more stamina you have, the longer you will be able to keep running before you begin to get out of breath.

2 *Strength tests*
If you want to try testing the strength of your arms and shoulders, you can do this by doing press-ups against a table. You need to use a table that will not move. Put your hands on the table and stand so that your feet are a comfortable distance away from the table, as in the illustration. Keep your body straight and bend your arms to that your chest touches the table. Straighten your arms and repeat. From 1 to 5 press-ups is not too good, the strength in your arms and shoulders could be improved. 5 to 10 press-ups is good but there is still room to improve. Over 10 is even better.

If you want to test the strength of you stomach muscles, lie on your back with your arms folded on your chest and legs out straight. Try to sit up smoothly with your head coming up first and your back curved, as in the illustration. If you can sit all the way up time after time, you are in good shape. If you can sit half-way up without effort that is not too bad. If you can hardly get off the ground, that is not very good.

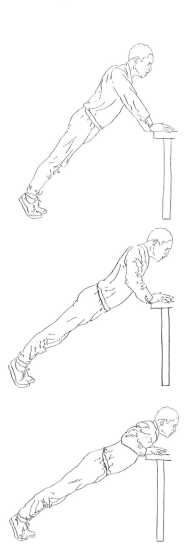

3 *Suppleness test*

If you want to test how supple you are, sit on the floor with your legs stretched out in front of you. Bend forward gently to touch your toes. Don't force yourself further forward than is comfortable. It is good, if you can hook your hands over your toes. It is not bad, if you can reach your ankles. But it is not so good, if you can only reach somewhere in between your knee and ankle.

What sort of exercise is for you?

It is quite likely that you get plenty of exercise.

All exercise has its problems!

Splitting yourselves into two groups, you could brainstorm why people like exercise and dislike exercise.

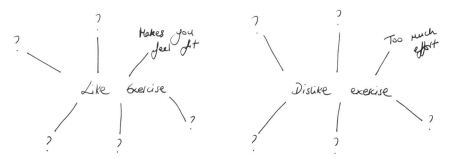

As a whole group compare your results. You could discuss in smaller groups whether you would like to take up more exercise. How would you set about doing this? One way might be to conduct a survey to discover what facilities are available for sport and exercise in your area.

All About Fats

❝ *When your time is up, it's up.* **❞**   **❝** *Who wants to be forty anyway* **❞**

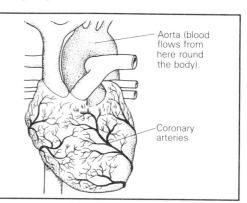

Look after your heart

Too much fat in the diet can damage blood vessels and lead to heart disease.

Heart disease is on the increase. It is the highest cause of death in this country. It is thought that 90% of 40 year-olds in Britain have diseased blood vessels. This damage is now being found in young children, although the effects are not usually seen until later in life.

Any fat that is not used for energy is stored as fat in the body, and can lead to weight problems.

Aorta (blood flows from here round the body).

Coronary arteries

❝ *I get plenty of exercise so, my heart's OK.* **❞**

A diet rich in fats, particularly saturated fats, can lead to heart and blood vessel disease. So, think about whether you are concerned at this stage in your life with the health of your body both now and for the future.

Many young people feel that they are not interested in issues like heart disease. Discuss your views on this in small groups: is it important to consider the amount of fat you eat now? Are you concerned about the possible effects on your future health?

Fats are needed by the body for energy, but most of us probably eat too much fatty food. Sometimes it is possible to choose foods with less fat in them. For each number in the list below tick which you would normally eat or drink, and then ring the choice you make for each food item.

Food	Tick	Choice
1 Ordinary bottled or carton milk	☐	A
Semi-skimmed milk	☐	B
Skimmed milk	☐	C
2 Thin-cut chips or French fries	☐	A
Crinkle-cut chips	☐	B
Thick-cut chips or oven chips	☐	C
3 Butter or hard margarine	☐	A
Polyunsaturated or soft margarine	☐	B
Low-fat spread	☐	C
4 Sausages, ordinary fried	☐	A
Sausages, ordinary grilled	☐	B
Low-fat sausages	☐	C
5 Cheddar cheese	☐	A
Edam or low-fat cheese	☐	B
Cottage cheese	☐	C

If your choices are mainly **A**, you are probably eating more fat than you have to. You could cut down on the fat you eat by choosing **B** foods.
If your choices are mainly **B**, your diet choices are better. You will be eating less fats in these foods, but you could reduce your fat intake further by turning to choice **C**.
If your choices are mainly **C**, you are doing the best that you can to cut down on the amount of fats eaten in these foods.
But remember even thick-cut and oven chips still contain a lot of fat and although low-fat sausages are better than normal sausages, they still contain a high level of fat.

Where does the fat we eat come from?

The sources of the fat that we eat in our diet today are shown in the following figures.

Dairy produce	Meat	Margarine and cooking oils	Other food
30% of fats	27% of fats	25% of fats	18% of fats

Saturated fats	Polyunsaturated fats
Much of the fat that we eat is saturated. It is mainly animal fats and a few vegetable fats. It is the saturated fats that damage the heart and blood vessels and which need to be cut down in our diet.	These fats are found mainly in vegetable products. It is better to eat these fats rather than saturated fat.

It is not always possible to have direct control over the type of fat that we eat. This is sometimes because we do not know what type of fat we are eating.

Some of your group could find out from the school or college canteen what type of fats and oils are used in cooking. Try to find out from you catering manager if saturated fats are used in cooking and frying. If these fats are used try to find out why this choice has been made. If the group is not happy with the type of fats used they could discuss ways in which changes might be made. It is possible that the catering manager is unaware of the harm that saturated fats can do to the body when eaten regularly in some quantity.

Hidden fats

Many foods contain quite high amounts of fat. Fat can be used by the manufacturer as a cheap filler in foods.

Other foods contain several different types of fats. Some are vegetable fats, which sound better but are very highly saturated.
The label shown here gives the list of ingredients for a packet of biscuits.

> Ingredients: sugar, rolled oats, wheatflour, *hydrogenated vegetable oil*, sugar solution, *palm oil*, skimmed milk powder, glucose syrup, salt, flavourings.

The ingredients in italic print are the saturated fats.

Think of ways in which people could cut down on the amount and type of fat that they eat, for example they could grill sausages rather than fry them. They could spread butter or margarine thinner. They could use polyunsaturated fats whenever possible, and lower fat alternatives.

Sugar and Salt

Sugars

Sugars are used by the body for energy but are not actually needed, because we can get the energy that we need from other carbohydrates, such as starch.

Try to think back. Have you always had a liking for sugar, or a sweet tooth? Sweets are often used as a treat or reward for young children. In a small group you could discuss your views on this. You might think about whether you treat yourself or whether other adults reward themselves with sweet food and bring this into your discussion.

Suppose you decide that you would like to cut down on the amount of sugar that you eat. In a group, brainstorm all the ways in which you could cut down on the amount of sugar in your diet. You might like to refer to your diet table from page 9 which should give you some idea as to when you eat sugar and the sort of foods in which it is found.

One of the problems with sugar is that like fat it can be hidden in the foods that we eat.

Brown and white sugar, molasses, treacle, golden syrup, and corn syrup are all a sucrose sugar. Other sugars are glucose, lactose, maltose, fructose or fruit sugar, honey, dextrose, glucose syrup and maple syrup.

If you look at the label below, which is from a packet of biscuits, you can see how manufacturers may try to hide sugars in their foods.

> Ingredients: milk chocolate, wheatflour, *sugar*, vegetable fats, *partially inverted refiners syrup, glucose syrup*, whole milk powder, salt, emulsifier, lecithin.

Fact box.

In an average diet 42.7kg of sugar is eaten by each person in this country in a year. This could amount to almost our own weight in sugar. It is estimated that of this amount, 16.7kg is added to food and drink by each person and the remaining 26kg is eaten in food that has sugar already added.
NACNE recommend that we should try to cut the amount of sugar eaten by half, which most people would find difficult.

ACTIVITY

You may like to do your own research to find out what types of foods contain sugars. You could check foods in your local supermarket or shop, and even some of the foods at home in the cupboard.

Working on your own or in pairs look at as many foods as possible. Include savoury foods as well as sweet. Try to find out if the manufacturers use different words which in reality all mean sugars. Don't forget to check soft drinks, canned drinks and juices.

When you have completed your research you could compare your findings in groups. Were there some unlikely foods that contained sugar?

In your discussions you might decide that you could cut down on the amount of sugar by adding less to drinks and food and also by using low sugar alternatives or artificial sweeteners. Another way to cut down the sugar eaten is to use foods and drink containing artificial sweeteners. Although this could reduce the amount of sugar that is eaten, it will not solve the problem of craving sweet foods. It is also possible to consume over the recommended daily allowance of artificial sweeteners, which is not advisable.

Salts

Salts are needed in small amounts by the body. Salt is widely used as a preservative and to flavour many processed foods.

Below you will find a number of statements about salt. Ring T or F to say whether you think each statement is true or false. Discuss your responses, working in pairs. The answers appear below.

		True	False
1	Babies need plenty of salt in their diet.	T	F
2	To keep our bodies healthy, the most salt we would eat is 6g or 1¼ tsps of salt per day.	T	F
3	Monosodium glutamate, sodium bicarbonate, sodium chloride, and baking powder all contain salts.	T	F
4	Foods that are kippered, cured or soaked in brine are all high in salts.	T	F
5	You can eat as much sea salt as you like, because it is natural and so is good for you.	T	F
6	Salt can contribute to high blood pressure.	T	F
7	Most people don't need to worry about the amount of salt that they eat.	T	F
8	Some people are more sensitive to salt than others.	T	F

Check your answers with those at the bottom of the page. You could discuss any points that you found interesting in your pairs or in groups.

A lot of salt is hidden in the foods that we buy. Think about the foods that you buy and eat that are high in salt. You could make a list like the one below to allow you to identify high- and low-salt foods where there is some choice.

High-salt foods	Low-salt foods
Salted nuts	Unsalted nuts, nuts and raisins
Crisps	Unsalted or low salt crisps
Danish Blue cheese	

Answers to statements

1 **False**   Babies get a certain amount of salt from the milk that they drink. Their kidneys can't cope with any extra salt. Baby foods should not have salt added to them even though to an adult the food could taste bland.

2 **True**   This is the maximum amount of salt recommended in our diet per day. In fact we only need half a gram or ⅛ tsp of salt a day.

3 **True**   These are all salts which means that they all contain sodium. So the salts that we eat are not just in the form of table salt, which is sodium chloride.

4 **True**   These are all ways of preserving foods by adding salt.

5 **False**   Sea salt has the same effect on the body as any other salt. It may contain other minerals but is basically no better for you.

6 **True**   If too much salt is eaten this can contribute to high blood pressure. High blood pressure can increase the chances of developing diseases, such as stroke, heart failure and kidney failure.

7 **False**   Most people eat far too much salt. It has been estimated that the average person eats 9 to 12 g of salt a day, the maximum amount being recommended is half this amount.

8 **True**   Some people are more sensitive to salt than others with an increased risk of developing high blood pressure. Unfortunately, individuals cannot be tested to find out if they are. It is much wiser for everyone to reduce the amount of salt that they eat.

So What Can We Eat?

By now you may be tired of hearing about foods that we eat too much of. So in this section we look at foods that are actually *good* for us!

Begin by working in small groups to brainstorm your ideas about the foods that are really good for us.

Compare the results of your brainstorm with the other groups. Have you included fruit and vegetables? What about the starchy foods, such as cereals, bread, pasta, etc?

Remember the NACNE report? It recommends that there should be an increase in the amount of fresh fruit and vegetables that we eat.

How much fruit and vegetables do you eat? Is this enough or could you eat more? Do you think that your intake of fruit and vegetables affects your health?

> Fruits are quick and easy to eat. Vegetables fresh or frozen should not be overcooked. In this way they keep their goodness and flavour.
> As well as being rich in vitamins and minerals, fruit and vegetables also contain fibre.

What about fibre?

You have probably heard people say that roughage or a high-fibre diet is good for you. Fibre also keeps the digestive system healthy, so that constipation and other bowel problems can be prevented.

You might like to have a rough guide to how much fibre you eat in your diet, by using the lists of foods shown opposite. Make a note of your meals for one day and then put A, B, C, or D against the foods that you have eaten and count up the totals.

A	B
Wholemeal bread	White rice
Brown rice	Pitta bread
Wholemeal pasta	White bread
Beans	Spaghetti
Peas	Pasta
Chapati	Nuts
Fibre-rich breakfast cereal e.g. Shredded Wheat	Dried fruit
	Sweet corn

C	D
Potatoes	Spinach
Carrots	Lettuce
Sweet potato	Cabbage
Parsnip	Tomato
Beetroot	Beansprouts
Swede & other root type vegetables.	Apples
	Banana & other fruits.

If you have had 4 to 6 helpings from groups A and B, then you have probably eaten a reasonable amount of fibre. If most of your fibre came from groups C and D, then you are probably not getting enough fibre in your diet.

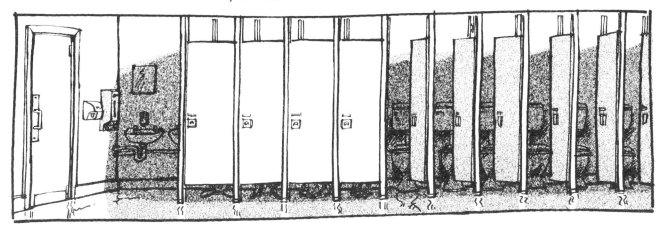

In Britain 4 out of 10 people suffer from constipation.

Many people, even some doctors, get embarrassed when talking about bowels, constipation, etc. Why do you think this is? Do you find it surprising that we have so many words to describe what is a normal bodily function. It *is* hard to talk about this subject without sounding coy or offensive.

So what is normal?

Ideally food should pass through the body quicky and the solid waste should be moist and bulky. The longer food takes to pass through the digestive system, the drier it becomes and the harder it will be to pass it out of the body. Straining to empty the bowels is not good. The amount of time taken for food to pass through varies according to what is eaten. A check on how long food takes to go through the body can be made by eating foods which show up in the solid waste, such as sweet corn or beetroot.

Good Es and Bad Es

You may have heard people say that you should not eat food if it contains E numbers. So just what are E numbers and is it true that we should not eat them? Start by finding out how much you know by answering these true or false questions in this quiz. For each statement, ring T if you think it is TRUE and F if you think it is FALSE.

		True	False
1	E numbers got their name from the EEC, which set up the code.	T	F
2	All foods that contain E numbers are bad for you.	T	F
3	E 102 is a colouring called tartrazine. People who suffer from asthma should not eat food or drink with it in.	T	F
4	Certain E numbers make foods keep for longer.	T	F
5	Some E numbers that we use in Britain are banned in the USA because it is believed that they are harmful.	T	F
6	All E numbers that are used are really needed in the food.	T	F
7	Some E numbers are natural products.	T	F
8	Foods have always had their E numbers listed on the food packet.	T	F
9	Not all food additives are E numbers.	T	F
10	Manufacturers have to list what flavourings they have used in the food.	T	F

You will find the answers below.

ACTIVITIES

» You could look at some foods, such as jelly, crisps, etc. to see if their flavour comes from natural flavourings or artificial flavours. For example, does the flavour of strawberry jelly come from strawberries?

» You could think more about colourings and flavourings by working in pairs. One of you should be A and the other B. A should argue in favour of artificial colouring and B against. Then swap over to argue about flavourings. A should argue against artificial flavourings and B for. (If you don't feel that you know enough on these subjects, you could do some research to prepare yourself for the arguments.)

1 True 2 False 3 True 4 True 5 True 6 False 7 True 8 False 9 True 10 False

Es to watch out for

Some E numbers have been found to cause harm to certain people who are sensitive to them. Some of these are summarized below:

E 102	Tartrazine	This is not suitable for some children and asthmatics.
E 110	Sunset yellow	This can cause skin rash and stomach upsets.
E 153	Carbon black	This may be linked to cancer and is banned in the USA.
E 210	Benzoic acid	This can cause skin rash, is not suitable for asthmatics and can cause stomach irritation.
E 220	Sulphur dioxide	This can cause irritation to the digestive system.

If you would like to add to the table above or find out more about E numbers and food additives there are two books which might help:

E for Additives Maurice Hanssen. Published by Thorsons.
E for Additives A Supermarket Shopping Guide Ed. Maurice Hanssen. Published by Thorsons.

Preservatives

Some E numbers or additives are preservatives which are useful to the food manufacturer to keep food fresh for longer. More foods are becoming available which don't contain preservatives. These foods will not last for so long. However, this does not cause any problems, if the foods are kept in suitable conditions and are sold by the right date.

Colour

Other additives may not be necessary. For example, some are only added to change the colour of food.

Many manufacturers use these colours, claiming that we want them, but do we? The food may look less attractive without these colours, but does that affect the flavour of the food? There are natural colours that can be used, but these are not as bright as the unnatural colours.

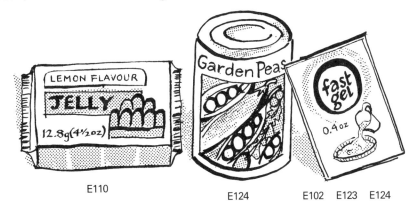

LEMON FLAVOUR
JELLY
12.8g(4½oz)
E110

Garden Peas
E124

fast gel
0.4oz
E102   E123   E124

Flavourings

Artificial flavours are also added to foods. The manufacturer does not have to state what flavours are used. Many flavours are made from chemicals and their recipes are top secret.

Big Business

One of the reasons we eat food that is full of fat, sugar, salt and additives, is because that's what we find in the shops. But why aren't the shops full of healthy food? Perhaps because the food industry is big business and like any other business, its main concern is with profits. So, what we eat has to be profitable to produce. But many people are very concerned about the methods of food production. At every stage from planting/rearing to selling, there are problems. Just a few of these problems are shown here but it's important to remember that there are two sides to every story. When you are reading through and discussing these examples, try to imagine what the food industry's defence would be in each case.

Using chemical fertilizers can reduce the long-term quality of the soil. The chemicals may also be washed away and pollute our rivers and drinking water.

Dangerous chemicals used to protect crops can be left in the food we eat. They can be very dangerous for farm workers and people who live near farms. They also kill harmless and/or useful creatures, such as butterflies, ladybirds and worms.

Bringing even more land into use, destroys the natural habitats of wild birds and flowers. There are less places in the countryside for people to visit. Soil erosion may also occur where too many trees and hedges are removed.

Very few animals are reared in the traditional way. Farmers are encouraged to produce high-fat animals, so there is less lean meat. The animals are injected with artificial hormones, which can be passed on to humans. Their living conditions can be cruel, especially for those birds and animals that are kept in confined spaces.

In Europe, government food policies often produce 'surpluses' – too much food for people to eat. These surpluses may be destroyed or stored in vast food mountains. This is expensive and adds to the cost we have to pay for these foods in the shops.

Poorer countries often have to import all their basic food, because they are encouraged to grow crops, such as sugar, tea and coffee for Western countries. Only the worst land is left for growing food for the people and the plantation workers are often paid very poor wages.

Much of the 'real value' of our food can be destroyed in the way it is processed. Many potentially harmful and/or unnecessary additives may be included. The 'profit value' increases sharply at this stage. For example, you can charge a lot more for a bag of crisps than for 1oz (25g) of potatoes.

66 I've enough problems without worrying about all this rubbish.99

Many of the people who feel concerned about these problems, believe that it is up to the Government to sort them out. Others believe that we need to do something ourselves. After all, *we* buy the food so that must give *us* some power. It's *our* money!

What do you think? These are some of the steps people take:

- Avoid buying certain foods.
- Choose alternatives, such as 'free range eggs'.
- Become vegetarian.
- Write to food manufacturers.
- Join a local conservation group.
- Join a pressure group, such as Friends of the Earth.

Discuss these ideas in a small group:

What do you feel about the problems?
Would you try any of these steps?
What good, if any, would it do?
Would you try anything else?

ACTIVITIES

≫ This activity will help you sharpen your ideas about some of the above problems. Work in pairs, taking it in turn to be *A* or *B*. *A* argues in favour of chemical fertilizers, *B* against. And so on, down the list of problems shown above.

≫ Find out more about food production by arranging to visit some relevant places, such as a farm, a dairy, a food processing plant, or an abbatoir.

≫ Find out more about food production and/or what you could do to help by writing to:

Friends of the Earth,
26–28 Underwood St,
London N1 7JQ

Compassion in World Farming,
20 Lavant St,
Petersfield,
Hants, GU32 3EW

You could also visit your local library to look at copies of appropriate magazines, such as *New Scientist*, *Nature* and *New Internationalist*.

Where Do We Eat?

If we want to change our eating habits, one of the first things we need to consider is where we eat.

At home

Most 16 to 19 year-olds live at home with one or more of their parents and this may make a change of eating patterns very difficult for anyone of this age. One point to consider is that food plays a major part in the balance of power within the home.

Mothers with little children put a great deal of time into cooking and persuading their children to eat what they prepare. Many toddlers would rather eat what *they* want and so food becomes an issue of authority. Many mothers feel that they should cook 'proper' meals, i.e. meat and two veg. Even when the family has grown up, the mother may feel that she is failing in her duty, if she doesn't provide the family meals. She may also feel that her authority is being challenged, if 'grown-up children' want to eat different food.

Taking this into account, discuss the situations described in these letters. What advice would you give the people who have written the letters?

- I've tried telling my family about the additives in food, but they think I'm crazy. My Dad does the shopping and he says he hasn't got time to start reading all the labels. Some of the stuff he buys is awful – more Es than anything else!

- I became vegetarian at 16 and at first my family thought I was mad. When they saw I was serious they stopped arguing, but my Mum started dishing up endless omelettes and cheese. Will it do any harm if I just eat these? What else could I do?

- My doctor says that I am overweight and should cut down on the food I eat, particularly on fats. I've tried talking to my Mum but it's hopeless. She cooks a big meal every evening but it's all the wrong things. How can I persuade her to let me eat something different?

ACTIVITY

Working in a group, start off by brainstorming the problems of eating at home *or* use the letters shown above. Up to 4 people should role play the parts of a family while the others act as observers. Play out a scene with a young person wanting to change what they eat. After 5 to 10 minutes, the observers should report on what happened. Then repeat the scene aiming for a more positive ending. Discuss the outcome. You could then try role-playing another scene related to an existing problem, using different members of the group.

Changing what you eat at home can be difficult whatever type of family you come from. In Britain there are many types of family. There may be one or more parent, and sometimes grandparents and other relatives too. And British families are based on a variety of cultural traditions. How far do you think these differences affect the amount of say young people have about what they eat?

Eating out

You do have more choice about what you eat outside of the home, but how healthy are the choices on offer? Things have changed and it is now possible to choose healthy food in many canteens and restaurants. But this is certainly not always the case.

Are you happy with what's on offer in your school/college/work canteen? You could keep a diary of the food that is served for one week and discuss whether it's really possible to make healthy choices. If you are not satisfied, you could arrange a meeting with your catering manager. It would be best to have clear ideas of what you would actually like changed. For example, you are more likely to meet with success if you ask for wholemeal sandwiches with cottage cheese, than if you simply complain that there's nothing but chips. You might also be able to persuade your local community dietician to come along to your meeting.

How about the food in local cafés and restaurants? Are the choices healthier where you are being charged a lot for your food? The choice in some fast-food outlets is very poor. Some national fast-food chains offer nothing that could be called low fat or high fibre, and use a lot of sugar and salt.

But again, things *are* changing and it's up to us as consumers not to spend our money in places where healthy choices are not available. That way, they'll have to change!

░▒▓ ACTIVITY ▓▒░

You could carry out a survey of what's on offer in your local area. Managers of local restaurants may be willing to talk to you and most places have a menu in the window. You may be able to advertise your findings in a local paper or on local radio or TV. Write to the paper or programme editor explaining what you are doing. They may be interested in interviewing you about your findings. Eventually, perhaps, you could prepare a leaflet as a guide to eating healthily in local restaurants.

Shopping on a **B**udget

Shopping for healthy food can be fun. But food isn't cheap and buying healthy food on a low budget requires a lot of skill.

Some people say that healthy food is no more expensive. Others argue that it is impossible to eat healthily on a low income or on social security. What do you think? Which of these foods would you say was more expensive?

White sliced bread	v	Wholemeal bread
Tinned peas	v	Fresh vegetables
Frozen chips	v	Potatoes
Butter	v	Vegetable margarine
Orange flavoured drink	v	Fresh oranges
Cakes and biscuits	v	Bananas
Meat pies/sausages	v	Chickpeas/kidney beans

It would seem that some healthy foods are cheaper than unhealthy options, but others are more expensive. So we need to consider the overall cost of a week's shopping. The following activity is designed to help you consider eating healthily on a low budget.

ACTIVITY

> Divide into groups of between 4 to 6 people.

> Each group should choose a type of household:
e.g. three students living in a flat,
a single parent with small child or an
Asian family of four.

> Divide your group into twos or threes. Call one lot *A* and the other *B*.

> The *A* group's task is to write a shopping list for the household for a week. The food can be anything that you think they would eat, without particularly considering health.
The *B* group's task is to write the list with health in mind. The food chosen must provide a healthy balance for the week.

> Visit your local shops and markets and price the items on your list, making a note of where the cheapest place is for each thing.

> Add up all the items on the list, so that you have a total cost for the week.

A and *B* can then compare results:

Which list is most expensive?
Which shops had the best offers?
Would it be possible to spend the total amounts if the household was on a low budget? (Check them against the latest social security payment averages. Remember to take into account rent, bills, etc.)

If you had to economize, which items would be left off the lists?
Were any of the items difficult to find?

> Discuss the results in the whole group. In particular:

What differences are due to the type of household you chose?
Do you now think it is possible to eat healthily on a low budget?

When you were visiting the shops and markets for the last activity, you may have found quite a lot of differences between them. Some shops, for example, stock products like low-fat cheese and milk. Others only offer the full-fat variety. And, of course, the prices can vary a lot from shop to shop. Even something as cheap as lentils can cost a lot if they are sold in a fancy packet or in tiny quantities. With some products we also need to think about freshness. Limp lettuces and soggy tomatoes don't make a very good salad!

Brainstorm all the ways you can think of, to get good value for money and variety from your local shops. For example:

● Shop around for the best offers.
● Buy in bulk and share with family/friends.
● Ask the manager to stock a particular item.

Often shops will change their buying patterns if we bring enough pressure to bear. They are in business to sell to us and they don't like losing customers. But sometimes individual criticism is not enough. Members of the community working together as a group may be more effective.

Discuss any changes that you feel it would be useful and possible for local shops to make. How might a community group encourage these changes?

A Variety of Tastes

In Britain it has become popular to eat a wide variety of diets and foods. Variations in diet can be caused by regional, national and cultural differences as well as for personal, religious and medical reasons.

The names of a range of diets are written around the globe in the margin. Would you add any more to complete the circle?

It can be interesting to look at other diets. They can add variety to the food we usually eat.

ACTIVITY

> You could find out about different diets by doing some research. For example, you might interview a family you know who eat an alternative diet. Work in small groups and think of the questions you would like to ask before you go to the interview. It would be valuable if the group as a whole could look at as wide a variety of diets as possible. You could do this by getting the small groups to look at different diets and then to report back to the whole group. In your report you could include recipes for and perhaps even some samples of food or an unusual meal.

If it is not possible to conduct interviews, you could find out from recipe books and restaurant menus about a variety of diets.

> When your groups have found out some details about different diets, you could look at your feelings about some of them. One way to do this is an agree/disagree activity. First brainstorm a list of statements about any diet you want to consider. Then make a space along a line in your room. Mark one end of the room 'Agree' and the other end 'Disagree'.

When the first statement is read out, individuals should place themselves along the line, depending on where they 'stand' on the statement. Talk to the person nearest to you to check why people are standing in that position. Afterwards move to a different position and see why people are standing there. Spend about one minute in each position and then move on to the next statement.

A little of what you fancy

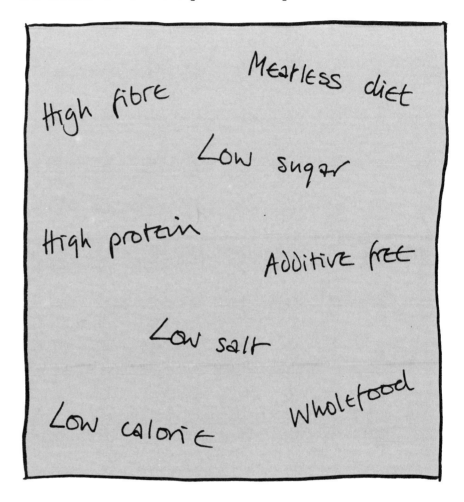

Messages about diet, like those above, can be confusing. Sometimes you might have got quite fed up reading all the dos and don'ts. It probably depends on your attitude to food.

Below you will see some statements about people's attitudes. In small groups you could discuss your feelings and views about these statements.

1 To keep healthy and live a long life you must stick rigidly to all the recommendations for a healthy diet.

2 I might as well eat what I like and enjoy myself. Who knows I might get knocked down by a car tomorrow.

3 Occasional unhealthy snacks will do the body no harm.

Work in small groups on a presentation to show how you feel *now* about food and diets. Your presentation could be in the form of a play, song or a mime which might be performed for the rest of the group. Other possibilities for display work could be: posters, a collage, or a logo for food and eating.